HOUSES &
HOMES

TIM WOOD

Viking

Acknowledgments

The publishers would like to thank Jonathan Adams, who illustrated the see-through scenes;
James Field, who illustrated the cover; and the organizations that have given their
permission to reproduce the following pictures:

Ancient Art & Architecture Collection: 20 top left.
Archiv für Kunst und Geschichte London Ltd/Erich Lessing: 15 top, 30.
Aspect Picture Library/Peter Carmichael: 27 bottom.
Bibliothèque Nationale de France: 27 top right, 28.
Bridgeman Art Library/Bibliothèque Nationale de France: 35.
British Museum: 8, 9 top, 38.
Cambridge University Museum of Archaeology & Anthropology: 9 bottom.
Domaine National de Chambord/Philippe Bricker: 31.
Werner Forman Archive: 15 bottom; right, **National Museum of New Zealand:** 37 left.
Robert Harding Picture Library: 5 bottom right, 5 top, 12 top, 12 bottom.
Michael Holford: 7, 10, 21 left.
Mansell Collection: 42.
Metropolitan Museum of Art/Rogers Fund & Edward S. Harkness Gift, 1920: 14.
Museum of London: 23 right, 23 left.
Museum of New Zealand: 36.
Scala: 21 right.
Science Photo Library/Peter Menzel: 44, 45 top, 45 bottom.
Science Museum/Science & Society Picture Library: 43 bottom.
Tokyo National Museum: 18.

Illustrators:
Jonathan Adams: Title page, 4–5 (small pictures),12–13, 14–15, 16–17, 24–25, 28–29, 32–33, 40–41.
Terry Gabbey (Associated Freelance Artists): 6–7, 8–9, 10–11, 22–23, 30, 35, 38–39,
Andre Hrydziuszko: 18–19, 26–27, 34, 36–37, 42–43, 44–45.
Kevin Madison: 4 (map), 34 (map).
Bill Donohoe: 20–21.
Richard Berridge (Specs Art): 31.
Richard Hook (Linden Artists): 46–47.
James Field: Cover.

VIKING
Published by the Penguin Group
Penguin Putnam Inc., 375 Hudson Street, New York, New York 10014, U.S.A.
Penguin Books Ltd, 27 Wrights Lane, London W8 5TZ, England
Penguin Books Australia Ltd, Ringwood, Victoria, Australia
Penguin Books Canada Ltd, 10 Alcorn Avenue, Toronto, Ontario, Canada M4V 3B2
Penguin Books (N.Z.) Ltd, 182-190 Wairau Road, Auckland 10 New Zealand

Penguin Books Ltd, Registered Offices: Harmondsworth, Middlesex, England

First published in Great Britain by Hamlyn Children's Books, 1995
First published in the United States of America by Viking,
a member of Penguin Putnam Inc., 1997

1   3   5   7   9   10   8   6   4   2

Copyright © Reed Educational and Professional Publishing Ltd., 1995

All rights reserved.

Library of Congress Catalog Card Number: 96–61761

ISBN 0-670-86777-2

Printed in Belgium

CONTENTS

HOUSES AND HOMES

The map below shows the locations of some of the main sites described in this book. The small illustrations show just a few of the many types of houses and homes that are built in different parts of the world and the great variety of building materials used.

In the last three-and-a-half million years, humans have migrated from their original birthplace in Africa to colonize almost every region of the world. The earliest humans lived by scavenging and hunting. They were wanderers who built temporary shelters when they needed them. It is only comparatively recently, when humans learned how to grow and store their own food, that they began to settle down and build permanent homes.

HOMES THROUGH HISTORY

The earliest homes were simple shelters. However, with the development of farming about 11,000 years ago, people no longer had to wander in search of food. Farming was a much more efficient way of obtaining what they needed. People who farmed were able to live in larger groups and to stay in the same place all the time. As tools improved, they also began to build bigger and better buildings. Groups of people worked together to build stronger defenses, more impressive palaces, and finer temples to honor their gods. They also began to decorate their buildings.

An igloo made of blocks of snow

Romany (gypsy) caravans, traveling homes in Europe

Crowded apartments in Hong Kong

Port Sunlight

Biosphere 2

Chambord

Çatal Hüyük

Sargon's Palace at Khorsabad

Yoshinogari

Copán

Mohenjo-Daro

Deir el-Medina

A wooden Dogon "men's house" with millet stalk roof in Mali, Africa

Hunza houses in northern Pakistan

Leaf houses in the African rain forest

The soft rock found in valleys in Cappadocia, Turkey, was hollowed out and used as shelters by Christians over 1,000 years ago. Paintings decorate the walls inside the caves.

DIFFERENT HOMES

People in different parts of the world built different types of homes. The homes they built depended on the climate, what materials were available, and their way of life. Climate has always been one of the main influences on housing. People who live in cold parts of the world design their homes to keep in the heat and keep out the wind, rain, and snow. People who live in hot parts of the world need protection from the sun, rain, and insects.

DIFFERENT MATERIALS

Climate also affected the materials that people used to build their homes. In hot places where it seldom rains, mud hardened by the sun has always been a useful building material. In cold places people have had to use more permanent materials such as wood or stone. In tropical areas where vegetation is lush, and where it is very wet, people have woven leaves to make waterproof homes that were easy to repair.

DIFFERENT SHAPES

Climate also influenced the design of houses. In cold regions people needed houses with sloping roofs so that rain and snow would slide off. In hot regions many people built their houses with small windows to keep the interior cool. These houses often had flat roofs, which were very practical in areas with low rainfall as they could be used as extra living areas. In swampy places or areas near rivers, people often built their houses on stilts to keep them out of the flood water.

INDUSTRIALIZATION

In the past, humans have built their houses out of the most abundant and easily worked local materials. For thousands of years, leaves, wood, mud, and stone were the most widely used building materials. The advances in technology made during the 18th and 19th centuries have brought enormous changes to housing. Materials such as bricks, steel, glass, concrete, and plastics are now produced on a wide scale and used in houses all over the world.

LIVING TOGETHER

This book examines how people living in different parts of the world have devised different ways of living together. Throughout their history, people have preferred to live in groups, deliberately building their homes on easily defended sites, near sources of food, water, and raw materials, on trade routes, or near places of religious significance. In the following pages you can discover some of the incredible variety of shapes and styles that people have used in the design of their houses and homes.

Houses on stilts are a common sight near the Mekong river in southern Cambodia (left). They are the safest form of housing in an area where the river floods each year. The water covers the fields with a layer of fertile silt.

A tepee (center left), a tent made by stretching buffalo hides over a framework of poles, was the home of the Plains Indians of North America. They could quickly pack up their tepees to follow the herds of buffalo they hunted. The concrete skyscraper (below) is now a common sight in most large cities where it provides high-density office and living space.

About 18,000 years ago, huts made from mammoth bones and tusks were built at Mezhirich, in the Ukraine. Few trees grow in this cold, windswept place. The bones and tusks of mammoths, killed by hunters with spears, clubs, and pitfall traps, must have been the most plentiful building materials available. A typical hut was 15 to 20 feet in diameter.

Early Stone Age people lived by hunting animals and gathering fruits, nuts, roots, tubers, and seeds. These hunter-gatherers had no permanent homes because their way of life forced them to move around, searching for food and following migrating herds of wild animals. They built temporary shelters when they needed them, and sometimes took refuge in caves.

LOCATION OF SITES

Hunter-gatherers chose the sites for their homes carefully. The best sites were near water, supplies of raw materials such as flint for making tools and weapons, and natural passages for trapping herds of wild animals. In some places, hunters built their homes close to grazing grounds or migration routes. Many migrating animals follow regular migration routes so the hunter-gatherers revisited old camp-sites season after season.

These shelters, built by reindeer hunters at Pincevent, in France, about 13,000 years ago, were made from branches and the skins of the animal the hunters killed. They looked very similar to the tepees of the Plains Indians of North America.

CAMPS

At certain times of the year, especially when the hunting was good, some groups of hunter-gatherers joined together and set up large camps. These were usually made at the narrow mouths of valleys where they could intercept migrating herds. Many camps were close to rivers that provided drinking water and fish. Some of the group probably remained near their camp, gathering food and fishing, while others hunted animals away from the camp.

BUILDING MATERIALS

To build their shelters the hunter-gatherers used whatever resources were plentiful and could be easily gathered. The most common materials were branches, rocks, leaves, and grasses. They worked all their materials by hand or with simple flint tools. In some places, the building materials came from the animals that were hunted, particularly hides and large bones.

Life inside a Gönnersdorf hut. Horse hides probably formed the roof and walls. Hides might also have been made into clothes after the hunters had chewed them to remove the fat and soften the leather.

HIDE TENTS

Many Stone Age hunters used the hides of animals to make tents. We know from archaeological remains that one group of reindeer hunters camped on the banks of the Seine river, in France, about 13,000 years ago. They built oval tents, using branches and reindeer skins. Some of them used flint scrapers to remove the fat from the skins. They stretched the hides to dry them, then sewed them together using bone needles, to make clothes and tents.

SHARED HOMES

About 10,000 years ago, at Gönnersdorf in Germany, a group of hunters built circular tents using wild horse skins stretched over a framework of poles stuck into the ground. The frames were strong enough to be left in place between visits. Many tiny crystal tiles engraved with simple figures of people, mammoths, horses, and birds have been found buried under the floors.

It seems that the settlement may have been occupied by two completely separate groups of people who lived there at different times of the year. One group lived in the tents during the winter. The other group, who may have been horse herders, lived there during the summer.

PORTABLE POSSESSIONS

Because Stone Age hunter-gatherers had to carry all their possessions when they traveled, they probably brought only what they needed for immediate survival. Their most important possessions included weapons, tools such as flint scrapers and bone needles, and furs for warmth and bedding. They had no furniture and probably sat on the ground, on logs, or on animal skins.

Reindeer provided not only meat and hides, but also antler. Antler was a valuable resource that could be carved into many useful objects, such as these harpoons for hunting fish.

7

This 14,000-year-old needle-making kit was found in France. It comprises a grooved antler, a polisher, needles, and stones for piercing.

Almost from the start of the Stone Age, over two million years ago, people found shelter in caves. Protected and warmed by their fires, these early humans left a record of their presence in the drawings and paintings found on the cave walls.

CAVE SITES

At one time it was thought that all people who lived in the Stone Age were cave dwellers. We now know that few groups actually were. This was partly because large caves, which are usually found in limestone rock, occur in relatively few places. Also, groups of hunter-gatherers soon used up all the food in an area. If people wanted to live in cave sites for a long period, they had to be near rivers or the sea, which provided a constant and plentiful supply of fish.

The main living area was in the front of the cave. We know from remains found in Stone Age hearths that our ancestors used fire to cook their food and to harden the points of wooden and antler-tipped spears. Beds were made by filling pits with springy vegetation, and coverings for the cave entrance were made out of hides or woven twigs.

THE ICE AGE

The main point of living in caves was for shelter from bad weather. Although the temperature inside a deep cave does not usually rise above 50°F, it will remain at about this temperature despite the weather conditions outside. Caves would have seemed comparatively warm places during the colder periods of the Ice Age. The inhabitants often made themselves more comfortable by building shelters in front of or inside the caves. Here they sat or lay on piles of grasses and leaves or animal skins, which cushioned them from the rocky floor.

FIRE

Caves also provided shelter from the wind, making it easier to light a fire by striking sparks with flints and rock containing iron. Fire kept wild animals away as well as providing light, warmth, and a means of cooking food. We are not quite sure when humans discovered how to make fire. Our earliest evidence shows that people living in China were using fire about 460,000 years ago. Cave dwellers also discovered that making a simple ring of stones, called a hearth, helped to control the fire and made the wood burn more efficiently. In many caves the hearth was located near the cave mouth, in the natural light.

THE FIRST BURIALS

Some time between 100,000 and 50,000 years ago, people called Neanderthals began to bury their dead in graves under the floors of caves. Some bodies were buried singly, others in groups. Many were buried with some possessions, such as flint tools, and items of food. This is the first sign that humans had begun to think about a life after death. The tools and food would be needed by the dead to lead their new lives. Burial of close relatives under the floor of a dwelling has been a common feature of many societies since this time.

CRO-MAGNONS

When the Neanderthals died out, other humans called Cro-Magnons began to flourish. About 30,000 years ago, the Cro-Magnons began to carve and paint on their cave walls. It is possible that these paintings had religious importance. The artists may also have believed that their paintings would bring good hunting, as many of the paintings were of animals.

THE FIRST PAINTINGS

Cro-Magnon artists achieved startling results with only simple methods and four basic colors. They painted with brushes made from animal hair, or blew colored powders—such as black charcoal, red ochre, or white chalk—through hollowed-out bones. Some paintings were simple hand shapes made either with a paint-covered hand or by blowing powders over the hand, leaving an outline, or "negative" picture. They also used natural bulges and dips in the rock to give their pictures form. Many paintings were created in underground chambers where there was no natural light. The artists must have used burning torches made from animal fat to see what they were doing. In some parts of the cave, they probably used tree trunks as ladders to reach high places.

There are over 230 caves, mostly in France and Spain, in which paintings have been found. The caves at Lascaux in France contain paintings of bulls and horses, the largest of which is about 18 feet long. Cave artists may have used stone lamps like the one below, found in France. A wick would have been floated in animal fat in the hollow.

An antler skull and harpoons. The skull may have been used as a kind of helmet or head-dress, probably for ceremonial purposes.

9

HOUSES IN ÇATAL HÜYÜK

This "Venus" figure found at Çatal Hüyük is probably a fertility symbol. Mother goddesses like this are very ancient. They represent the creative power of nature. Their worshipers believed mother goddesses could give good harvests and large families.

Making bricks for a new house at Çatal Hüyük. Living in a house in Çatal Hüyük must have been like living in a cave, since most buildings did not have windows. The walls of the finished houses were decorated with paintings and statues of fertility goddesses and animals.

About 10,000 years ago, some groups of people in the Middle East discovered how to grow crops and tame animals. Their wandering life was over. They settled down near their fields and built permanent homes. With more reliable food supplies and better homes, these first farmers now had time to learn other skills, such as weaving. They made new tools, such as sickles for cutting cereals, hand mills for grinding the grain into flour, and pots for storing food. They also learned how to build strong stone walls and to make bricks out of mud.

THE FIRST TOWNS

Soon people began to gather into larger settlements for protection. They worked together to build public storehouses to hold grain supplies, and traded their food surpluses with other communities.

The earliest town was probably Jericho, which was built in about 8000 B.C. This important trading center was defended by strong walls over 12 feet high and six-and-a-half feet thick. The town of Çatal Hüyük, which was built about 1,000 years later in what is now modern Turkey, had a different form of defense that may have been more effective than Jericho's famous walls.

ÇATAL HÜYÜK

The 6,000 inhabitants of Çatal Hüyük were Stone Age farmers and traders. They built their town near a river and used the water to irrigate their land. Each house at Çatal Hüyük was constructed around a strong wooden framework, the timbers of which were shaped with stone tools. The walls were built from mud bricks that had been made in wooden molds and dried in the sun. The builders used mortar made of sticky mud to hold the bricks together. The walls were then covered with a thick layer of daub—mud that was mixed with straw to bind it together.

A TOWN WITHOUT STREETS

Çatal Hüyük had very few open spaces and no streets. The houses were built next to each other, each one sharing its walls with neighboring buildings. The inhabitants reached their own homes by clambering over the roofs of other houses. Once there, they went in though the main entrance, which was a hole in the flat roof, and down a ladder into the main room. The houses had no ground-floor windows. Inside they were probably cool, although rather airless. The inhabitants had few pieces of furniture, but they regularly redecorated the interiors of their homes by painting the walls.

ORDER OUT OF CHAOS

At first sight the design of the town looks disorganized. Many houses were built on the ruins of earlier dwellings that had collapsed. This meant that roofs were at different heights. However, there was actually a good deal of order to the design. The bricks were made in sizes based on the standard length of a human hand and foot. Many of the houses were standard sizes too—about 20 feet long by 15 feet wide. Other details, such as doorways and hearths, were also very similar. Some of the open courtyards were used as places for leaving trash.

STRONG DEFENSE

Although there was no perimeter wall as there was at Jericho, Çatal Hüyük was by no means unprotected. The design of the houses was a useful form of defense. Once the wall of a town protected by perimeter walls is broken, the whole town will probably be captured. But at Çatal Hüyük, attackers who broke into one of the walls of the outer houses would have been faced with a bewildering maze of other walls. Interestingly, while the famous Bible story describes the destruction of Jericho's walls, there is no archaeological evidence that Çatal Hüyük was ever captured.

This scene shows how the buildings at Çatal Hüyük might have looked. Remains found at Çatal Hüyük suggest that the town became rich through trade. A black rock called obsidian was one of the most important imports. The town may also have been a religious center.

MOHENJO-DARO

This game board was found at Mohenjo-Daro. It appears to be for a kind of chess game. The fact that the inhabitants had time to play games like this indicates that their society was probably wealthy.

Very little evidence of furniture or other household objects has survived from Mohenjo-Daro. The reconstruction of the house shown below is based on remains of the buildings and much guesswork about how the Mohenjo-Darans lived.

The pierced pot (below) probably held scent and may have been used as an air freshener.

As humans improved their farming techniques, their communities grew larger. Great cities developed along the banks of large rivers, such as the Nile in Egypt and the Tigris and Euphrates in Sumeria. One of the best-planned cities was the Harappan city of Mohenjo-Daro, which was built near the Indus river about 2000 B.C. Mohenjo-Daro, which contained about 40,000 people, was very rich, probably because of the valuable grain that was stored inside its walls.

THE HOUSES

The lower part of the city was where most of the population lived. Most houses there were rectangular and up to 1,500 square feet. They had foundations and outer walls made of fired bricks held together with mortar. Fired bricks, which had been baked in large ovens, were much harder and lasted longer than sun-dried bricks.

The walls were up to 15 feet high and were built around frames made from wooden beams. Regularly spaced recesses in the tops of the wall suggest that the beams were slotted into the brickwork, helping to support the walls.

ACCOMMODATIONS

Many houses were two stories high and large enough to hold an entire family, several guests, and servants. The houses were designed to be as cool as possible inside. They had few windows, most of which were covered with crossed bars, or sheets of alabaster (a stone that can easily be split) or terra-cotta (a form of pottery).

Many houses had open central courtyards, overlooked by rooms with balconies. These courtyards were probably used for doing domestic chores and as children's play areas. Only a few of the houses had outside windows, and most had just a single door that opened onto the street. These arrangements kept the houses secure, cool, and free from dust.

PLUMBING

The people of Mohenjo-Daro probably had sanitary houses because the city had one of the earliest known public drainage systems. Many houses had their own bathrooms. Fresh water was supplied to the houses by brick tunnels. Once used, the water was carried to the main city drains through gutters built near the walls of the houses. A network of clay pipes and underground drains carried water and waste out of the city. At some crossroads, there were places for dumping trash.

Here may delight be thine through wealth and children. . . . Remain here now, never to depart; enjoy the full measure of thy years playing with sons and grandsons. Be glad of heart within thy home.

— A marriage blessing —

THE GREAT BATH

Mohenjo-Daro also had a bathhouse, which was located in the upper part of the city. The building contains a sunken pool about 40 by 23 by 8 feet, which was made watertight with bricks, mortar, and bitumen. The Great Bath may have been used for ritual cleansing during religious ceremonies conducted by the city's ruling priests.

There is much we do not know about the Indus Valley people. From the meager evidence of ruins and a few objects, we do know that the civilization at Mohenjo-Daro lasted for over 300 years and that the city was abandoned about 1700 B.C.

Bricks at Mohenjo-Daro may have been made in kilns similar to this one (top). Bricks were piled in a beehive-shaped mound and a fire was lit underneath. Finished bricks were laid in horizonal rows (above). The pattern of bricks in these rows is called a bond.

The straight streets, regular houses, and evidence of a police force suggest that Mohenjo-Daro was a well-ordered, highly organized society. Gutters ran under the streets, carrying water and waste away from the houses (far left). Brick toilets (the earliest known) were a feature of many houses (left).

13

A model of an Egyptian house. Models of buildings, people, work scenes, and food were often put into tombs. They represented the real versions, which it was believed could be used in an afterlife.

By about 3000 B.C., the pharaohs in Egypt ruled over one of the largest and most powerful empires in the world. The workers who made the pharaohs' elaborate tombs lived, worked, and died in a village built especially for them.

DEIR EL-MEDINA

Deir el-Medina was home only to highly respected craftworkers and their families. Compared to the country's peasant farmers, the workers were much richer and lived in comfort. Many pottery fragments covered with hieroglyphics have been found at Deir el-Medina, suggesting that its inhabitants were also better educated than most Egyptians.

The village was surrounded by a wall 430 by 164 feet. Inside this enclosure were 70 houses, while outside there were another 50.

THE HOUSES

Houses at Deir el-Medina were packed tightly together in terraces without gardens. A typical house was similar in style to houses in other Egyptian villages but was larger, measuring about 33 by 10 feet. It had rough stone foundations about 2 feet high, on top of which were walls made of mud bricks. The house had a flat roof that was reinforced by beams made from the trunks of palm trees, and supported by a large pillar.

Each house had a single entrance that opened onto an alley. The doorway, which was painted red, was inscribed with the name of the villager and may have been covered to protect the occupants from the sun. In order to keep the interior cool, the house had only a few windows.

This tomb painting shows Egyptian metalworkers like those at Deir el-Medina. Most of the craftworkers there helped build the pharaohs' tombs in the Valley of the Kings.

INTERIORS

Most of the houses in Deir el-Medina were similar inside, with public and private rooms, an outside kitchen, and at least one cellar. The internal walls were plastered and painted white. Some were decorated with paintings. The floors were made of hard-packed earth.

The villagers of Deir el-Medina were rich by the standards of the day. The craftworkers were paid each month in goods, usually grain, but also fish, oil, and linen. They received bonus payments of salt, wine, meat, and even silver.

> **Do not let your conduct in the house be too high-and-mighty, and never lord it over your wife. . . . Do not say to her "Where is so-and-so? Bring it here" when she has put it away carefully in some safe place.**
>
> —— *Egyptian inscription* ——

PUBLIC ROOMS

The first room off the street was a public room used for receiving visitors and for religious ceremonies. It contained a shrine at the top of a short flight of steps, where the women of the house made offerings. The second room was larger and usually lit by a high window. The main item of furniture was a built-in couch. In some houses a shrine was hidden behind a false door in the walls of this room.

PRIVATE ROOMS

Behind the two public rooms were two or more private rooms. These were used mainly as bedrooms, and contained headrests for sleeping on and storage chests for clothes and valuables. At the back of the house was a kitchen with all the utensils needed for preparing meals, such as grindstones, kneading boards, water jars, and an oven. Many kitchens had a trellis roof that gave protection from the sun. Stairs led down to a cellar that was used for storage and, in some cases, as a family tomb.

The Egyptians decorated their furniture with precious stones, ivory, metal, and mother of pearl. Many Egyptian chairs had legs shaped like lions' paws. This chair, found in the tomb of an Egyptian queen, is also covered with thin sheets of gold.

15

SARGON'S PALACE

The see-through scene on these pages shows part of Sargon's palace. Most of the building was made from simple mud bricks. Harder, kiln-baked bricks were used to form archways and were glazed in different colors to create decorative panels. Wood from cedar, cypress, juniper, and maple trees was used to make roof beams and gates. Part of the palace was dominated by a seven-tiered ziggurat that towered over the seven main temples, each dedicated to a different Assyrian god. The king took part in many religious rituals when he was in residence.

One of the most magnificent buildings of the ancient world was the palace of the Assyrian warrior king Sargon II. Built as part of the new city of Khorsabad, in what is now Iraq, the walled palace was truly fit for a king. It was over 160,000 square feet, and contained 209 rooms. The palace was built on a raised platform and towered over the landscape. The platform and much of the palace were built with mud bricks. These were laid before they were completely dry, so that the whole structure solidified under its own great weight.

THE KING'S APARTMENTS

A series of courtyards, the largest of which was over 8,000 square feet, divided the palace into three main areas—the king's apartments, the state chambers, and a temple area. The king's apartments were luxurious. The floors were decorated with patterned pavements, although in many parts there were mats and even carpets.

When the king was not away at war, he enjoyed eating magnificent banquets. Some of the guests lounged on couches. Others sat on chairs and ate from tables. Servants fanned the diners constantly with large fly whisks made of woven reeds.

THE STATE CHAMBERS

The state chambers contained guest suites for visitors, such as ambassadors from other lands. The walls and corridors were decorated with stone reliefs and murals. These showed the exploits of the king in battle, the Assyrians' victories, and the punishments given to their enemies. The murals were designed to impress and terrify visitors.

The palace had several bathrooms. Each contained at least one bath and a toilet. An Assyrian bath was a terra-cotta tub big enough to sit in. Slaves heated the bathwater in bowls that stood on a hearth or brazier in a corner of the room. A chimney hood above the fire carried away the smoke. The toilet consisted of two raised foot stands with a drain between. Brick drains, coated in bitumen to make them waterproof, carried the waste to underground sewage pipes.

THE ABANDONED PALACE

Sargon lived at the palace for only part of the year, resting from battle, receiving ambassadors, and ruling his empire. As king, it was his sacred duty to wage war against neighboring countries. For most of the spring and summer, he was away on campaign. When Sargon was killed in battle, his son Sennacherib abandoned the largely unfinished city and its palace.

1   Ziggurat
2   Temple of moon god Sin
3   Private apartments
4   Throne room
5   Royal apartments
6   Reception room
7   Bathroom
8   Sewage pipe

The section of the palace shown below contained the state chambers and private apartments. The largest room here was the throne room, which was 150 feet long. Here Sargon received important visitors and gave orders to his officers. Sargon's throne was raised on a stone platform.

The palace also contained a great many storerooms for holding the vast amounts of tribute sent by defeated countries. A number of rooms contained thousands of clay tablets on which state records were kept. Scribes labored almost constantly recording the king's words, and a number of offices equipped with clay benches were set aside for this work.

HOMES OF THE YAYOI

The Yayoi made fine clay ceramics. This elegant but practical pot was shaped on a potter's wheel. The neck is decorated with the mask of a human face.

Thatch provided a warm and waterproof covering for the roofs of Yayoi houses. Thatch is also safer if the roof collapses, as often happpened in this earthquake zone.

Protection from raiders was a high priority for the inhabitants of early farming settlements in many parts of the world. For thousands of years, walls and ditches were the most popular means of defending homes and the wealth of a settlement. The remains found at Yoshinogari in southwestern Japan, built over 2,000 years ago, show it was a fine example of a fortified farming village.

YOSHINOGARI

The inhabitants of Yoshinogari were Yayoi. These farmers were the first Japanese to live in permanent settlements. They grew rice and built villages near rivers, and on the plains near the coast of Japan. The settlement of Yoshinogari was surrounded by a moat and a wooden palisade nearly 3,000 feet long. Around the edge of the settlement were several high watchtowers, which suggest that the Yayoi lived in troubled times. The palisade was obviously designed to defend the village.

THE BUILDINGS

Within the palisade, there were two main types of buildings—homes and store-houses. The oval houses were made mainly of wood and thatch, although some had stone walls. They were between 16 and 23 feet long, and 15 to 20 feet wide. Many of the houses did not have separate walls and roofs. Instead the whole building was supported on four sturdy posts.

The spaces between these pillars were filled in by beams bound with ropes. The whole structure was draped with a sloping thatched covering made of reeds, which came right down to the ground. The shaping of the beams, and use of precise joints, indicate that the Yayoi used iron tools.

FLOORS AND WALLS

The floors of the houses were shallow pits dug in the ground. This type of floor is found in many parts of the world. In some places, pits are used instead of high side walls. In other places they are dug down to create a firm foundation for the floor.

The floors of some Yayoi dwellings were dug so deep that the inhabitants needed ladders to get in and out of their houses! The earth of the floor was beaten to make a level surface. In the center of each house was a clay fire pit. Around the edge of the house was a raised earth bench held together with wooden planks. This acted as a seat, and also prevented groundwater from seeping under the walls.

OTHER BUILDINGS

Some of the houses were much larger than others, and may have belonged to richer people in the village. Although there is little direct evidence that powerful priests or rulers lived in the village, one grave found at Yoshinogari is bigger than the others, and might have belonged to a king.

Some of the buildings were raised on wooden posts and were taller than the houses. These were not homes but storehouses. Many of them had wooden "collars" fixed to the posts, to prevent rats getting at the rice and grain. Others had cleverly carved ladders leading up to the doors, which were shaped to make it impossible for rats to climb.

Archaeological evidence shows that Yoshinogari (shown reconstructed below) must have had towers where guards could watch the surrounding countryside and give warning of attack. We know the village suffered at least one attack because nearby are hundreds of graves containing the skeletons of people who met violent deaths, probably in battle.

Steps (top) may have been used to reach the storehouses. The shape makes it hard for rats to climb up. Accurate joints (above) helped to make the wooden walls strong and weatherproof.

ROMAN APARTMENTS

Roman plumbing was very advanced. The Romans had water pumps, pipes, and faucets similar to the one shown here. Only the richest people had water piped to their own houses.

Insulae were designed simply to accommodate as many people as possible in the least amount of space. In this block you can see the poorest apartments at the top and the better rooms and shops below.

Ancient Rome and many other cities in the Roman Empire contained marble palaces, triumphal arches, stadiums, and other impressive public buildings. But the glories of these buildings often hid the squalor of the tall apartment houses and densely packed slums in which most citizens lived. Many ordinary Roman citizens lived in cramped rooms in constant fear of fire, collapsing walls, and other dangers.

ORDINARY CITIZENS

Nearly 70 million people lived in the Roman Empire. The richest owned majestic palaces or luxurious villas. Many had large gardens, running water, indoor bathrooms, central heating, glass windows, and beautiful mosaics and wall paintings.

But most ordinary citizens could only afford to live in small apartments in tall buildings called *insulae*. There was no piped water or toilets, so people had to visit public baths to wash, and go to public lavatories. Water for cooking and drinking had to be carried from the public fountains. Rents were high and people crammed into the small rooms to save money.

> But here . . . we live in a city that's propped up with matchsticks. . . . That's the way the landlord stops the building from falling down, papering over the cracks in the old walls, telling us not to worry, to sleep easy, and all the time the place is about to collapse around us.
>
> —— *Juvenal* ——

DEATH TRAPS

The ground floors of the insulae were built from brick or stone held together with lime mortar. Above these were upper stories built of wood and plaster, supported by wooden beams and reached by steep wooden staircases. Brick arches were used for door and window openings. Most windows had shutters but no glass. Although there were some limits on the height of insulae—normally only five stories were allowed—there were few controls over the actual building, and standards could be low. Often the cheapest materials were used. There are many reports of insulae collapsing and killing or injuring the inhabitants.

STOREFRONT BUILDINGS

In most Roman cities, the ground floors of the insulae were taken up with stores that sold a variety of goods. The stores were also workshops where the shopkeeper made the goods that were on sale. The upper stories of the insulae overhung the ground-floor stores and were supported on rows of columns, which made a sheltered walkway for shoppers.

DANGER FROM ABOVE

The insulae had no drains or trash cans, so people threw their garbage out of the window into the street below. The Roman poet Juvenal complained about the dangers that could come from these upper stories, including falling tiles and pots. "People will think you stupid," he wrote, "if you go out to dinner without making your will first. Every open window can spell sudden death to the passer-by. So you just hope and pray they decide to throw out nothing more harmful than a brimming chamber pot."

Insulae were heated with wood-burning braziers that were unpleasant and dangerous to use because the apartments had no chimneys. The insulae were crowded together and contained a lot of wood, which created a fire risk. Most Roman towns had their own fire brigade, called vigiles. *In Rome there were seven brigades, each with 1,000 firefighters. The firefighters collected water in leather buckets from public fountains and pools. They also used small hand-held pumps, but these could not squirt much water.*

Lighting in Roman houses was provided by oil lamps made of pottery or bronze (like the one pictured below left). The lamps gave very little light.

Most Romans used chests to store their linen and clothes. Wardrobes, like the one shown below, were owned by the wealthy.

ANGLO-SAXON HOUSES

No one really knows exactly what Saxon houses looked like. We do know that the Saxons were skilled woodworkers who could cut complicated joints and who used pegs to fix wood together. The scene below shows how Saxons may have built a house. In the background, workers are cutting radial planks. The pit was probably there to keep the floor timbers dry.

In the fifth century, members of many different German tribes, including the Angles and Saxons, moved into parts of what had been the Roman Empire. Some of them settled in Holland, while others crossed the North Sea and settled in eastern Britain.

WOODEN WALLS

The first Anglo-Saxons to arrive in Britain lived in villages. In some places, they used stone from old Roman buildings to build their houses. In other places they added wooden extensions to existing Roman buildings. But in most places, the Anglo-Saxons built new houses out of wood that they cut from the surrounding forests. They felled the trees with iron axes and split the tree trunks lengthwise with wooden wedges to make planks. Planks split this way are much stronger than sawn planks.

Each building in the village was made from planks fastened with wooden pegs to a stout framework of wooden posts. The planks were slightly wedge-shaped and interlocked to form an even surface that kept drafts out. Windows were simple openings that could be covered by shutters in bad weather.

ROOFING

The Anglo-Saxons thatched their roofs with grasses or reeds that grew on river banks. First they put a light wooden framework on the roof, which was pitched to keep off the rain. Over this they laid bundles of reed stems cut to length. The reeds were held in place with hazel pegs called braunches. Thatch is an excellent roofing material that is still used today in many parts of the world. It is light and waterproof, and keeps in the warmth. There is no evidence to show that the Saxons had chimneys or smoke holes in their roofs. If they did not, the interiors of their houses must have been very smoky. Skeletal remains show that many Anglo-Saxons suffered from blocked noses, which might have been caused by the smoke.

INSIDE THE HOUSES

Houses were often built so that their doors and windows faced south to maximize the light inside. Each house was built over a pit which was probably designed to keep the wooden floorboards dry. Inside, the furniture consisted of wooden tables, benches, and stools. Beds were basically wooden boxes filled with animal furs and wool blankets. A small fire in a sand-filled firebox provided heat and some light. At night they used candles made from animal fat. About 10 family members of all ages lived in each house. When the house became too run-down to live in, they simply built a new one in a different part of the village.

Waterlogged remains found in modern Germany prove that some Anglo-Saxon houses had outer and inner walls made from wattle panels. From other remains we know that animals were kept indoors. Some houses had internal enclosures that could hold over 20 cattle. Most Saxon houses were roofed with reed thatch (right). Wooden shingles (below right) might have been split from straight-grained wood to make waterproof tiles for some halls.

FAMILY GROUPS

Each village was home to several different families who may have been distantly related. In the village each family group of about 30 people had its own hall that was a meeting place and the place where the family went to eat most of their meals. Around each hall were houses, used mainly for sleeping, and workshops that were shared by the family group. The workshops were used for weaving wool and linen cloth, and for other craftwork, such as carving bone and antler.

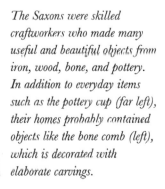

The Saxons were skilled craftworkers who made many useful and beautiful objects from iron, wood, bone, and pottery. In addition to everyday items such as the pottery cup (far left), their homes probably contained objects like the bone comb (left), which is decorated with elaborate carvings.

HOMES IN A MAYAN CITY

The scene below shows two houses belonging to one Mayan family living in Copán. On the left is a sleeping house, and on the right is a kitchen house. The Mayans spent what little leisure time they had outdoors or in the ceremonial center of the city. In many places, including Copán, where there was a shortage of building stone, the Mayans made the walls of their homes out of wattle and daub.

The Mayan civilization flourished in the Yucatán peninsula in Central America between A.D. 300 and 900. They built great stone cities where they worshiped their gods. Copán, one of the greatest Mayan ceremonial centers, contained huge pyramids and temples, and palaces where the ruling classes lived. However, most of the city's people were farmers who lived in dozens of villages scattered in the surrounding jungle. They came to the ceremonial center only on market days or to take part in religious festivals.

THE HOUSES

Each peasant family had one or two houses, which stood on a small plot of land surrounded by a dry stone wall. Houses could be round, square, or rectangular, and were sometimes rounded at both ends. The building stood on rubble foundations and had high-pitched roofs to keep off the heavy tropical rains.

The walls and roofs of the houses varied from place to place. In jungle areas, roughly shaped wooden planks or posts were commonly used for the walls, and palm leaves for the roofs. In highland areas, the sturdy walls were made with stones picked from the ground and stuck together with lime mortar. Thatched roofs were common. The Mayans shaped all the building materials they used with stone or obsidian tools.

INTERIORS

Some families had two houses. They used one for sleeping and one for cooking and eating. Families with only one house divided it into two parts with a wall. Most houses had a single entrance. A curtain of string tied with copper bells was hung in the opening. The bells jingled when anyone tried to enter the house. The kitchen had an open fire on the floor. This was contained in a hearth made from three large stones that supported a flat ceramic baking dish. The smoke from the fire escaped through the thatch. At Copán, water was fetched from the nearby river in pots. Many other cities did not have a convenient river nearby, so the Mayans dug underground cisterns or built reservoirs to store rainwater.

THE SLEEPING ROOM

On the floor of the sleeping room were low beds or sleeping racks made from small branches laced together and covered with woven grass mats. The Mayans used the cotton cloaks they wore, which were called *mantas*, as blankets. They buried their dead under the dirt floors of their houses, perhaps to keep the spirits of their ancestors close by. After several burials, or when the house became too rundown to repair, the building was abandoned and treated as a sacred burial plot.

1. **Sleeping house**
2. **Bed**
3. **Kitchen house**
4. **Buried ancestor**
5. **Foundation made of rubble**
6. **Plastered stone walls**
7. **Thatched roof**
8. **Tomb in temple**
9. **Bees' nest provides honey**

The heart of Copán was a massive religious center dedicated to the gods of weather, crops, and animals. In the center of the city was an "acropolis," a gigantic raised stone platform on which stood a number of important pyramids and temples. The Mayans probably used professional builders or even architects to build their temples, pyramids, and palaces. We know they drew plans for some of their buildings on paper and wood. In contrast, the Mayans made no real effort to plan the outer parts of their cities. The houses of ordinary people were probably just built by family members helping each other.

LIFE IN A MONGOL YURT

The Mongols used long poles to spread the sheets of felt over the roofs of their yurts. These homes could be put up or taken down in a matter of minutes. They were ideal for tribes whose lifestyle required them to follow their herds as they moved from place to place in search of fresh grazing.

By about 1200, people in most parts of the world lived in cities, towns, or villages. But in Mongolia, one group of wandering herders, known as the Mongols, hated city life and despised peasant farmers. At the same time they envied the wealth of the city dwellers, and set out to conquer and plunder the rest of the world. Wherever they went, the Mongols took their houses—squat tents called "yurts"—with them. They even chose their allies by whether or not they lived in yurts. Their leader, Genghis Khan, called himself the "ruler of all tribes who live in felt tents."

NOMADS FROM THE STEPPES

The Mongol tribes were divided into "oboks," or clans. Clan members lived in scattered family groups, each with its own grazing land. The Mongols' nomadic (wandering) way of life followed a pattern of seasonal migration. After spending the winter in sheltered valleys, each clan moved with its herds of sheep, horses, and cattle to grazing lands on the high plateau of the steppes for the summer. Because they needed to stay with their animals, the Mongols did not have permanent settlements. Instead, each family group lived in a collection of squat circular tents called "yurts" or "gers." Their animals were kept in nearby pens at night or allowed to graze on the steppes.

YURTS

A yurt was made of a thick felt cover that was stretched over a light wooden frame. The floor was made of wooden planks, in the center of which was a pole that held up the roof of the tent. Next to the pole was a stove or firebox for cooking and providing warmth, with a chimney that poked out through a hole in the roof.

Rugs were hung up around the wall for decoration and to help keep the yurt warm. Arranged in a circle against the wall were beds, and the cupboards and chests that held the family's possessions and staples. The entrance usually faced south. This allowed the maximum amount of light in and kept out the cold Mongolian winds that blew mainly from the north.

ON THE MOVE

Yurts made ideal homes for nomads. They could easily be taken down, the felt rolled up, and the framework dismantled in about an hour. But by 1200, many Mongols used wooden carts to transport their yurts. Each yurt was lifted in one piece onto a cart. Mongol women stood in the entrance to the yurt, and drove the teams of oxen that pulled the carts.

While on campaign, Mongol soldiers practically lived in the saddle, carrying all their possessions in leather sacks strapped to their horses. They ate mare's milk that had curdled in the sun. Their main drink was fermented mare's milk, called *kumiss*. Raw meat was often placed under the saddle of a horse to tenderize it.

AT WAR

The Mongols despised city dwellers and often destroyed the cities they captured. When the Mongol armies poured into China and Europe, their yurts traveled in great hordes behind them, like fleets of ships carrying the families across the land.

In China, the Mongol leader Kublai Khan built a new capital city, then called Ta-tu, and now known as Beijing. But even there, in the heart of the Imperial city, the walls of Kublai Khan's sleeping quarters were hung with carpets, rugs, and silks so they resembled the inside of a yurt. Many important Mongol officials and members of the royal family preferred to sleep in yurts in the palace gardens, rather than in their official quarters.

Inside a Mongolian yurt. Although the furniture and possessions are modern, the interior of this yurt would have seemed very familiar to a Mongol living in the time of Genghis Khan.

TIMBER-FRAMED HOUSES

The builders often built sections of the frame in the woods where they felled the trees. At the site they assembled all the pieces and hauled them into position with ropes and pulleys.

A medieval upstairs toilet was just a seat with a hole in it.

During the Middle Ages, many houses were built using timber frames. Wood was plentiful and easy to work. The different parts of the frame, the walls, roof, and floors could be joined together so that the whole building was like a giant box. It was a practical and effective design that became popular all over Europe.

MAKING THE FRAME

Timber-framed houses were made in sections so they could be put up quickly and easily. Oak was favored because it is very strong and resists rotting, and huge areas of oak forest were cut down for their timber. The craftsmen cut the timbers to length and shaped them using saws, axes, and planes. They used different types of joints to connect the different timbers.

PUTTING UP THE FRAME

Once they had cut the timbers according to the plans they had made, the builders marked all the timbers so that they knew where each piece fitted. They carried the timbers to the site and fitted them together to make the sections of the framework. The timbers were locked into their joints with wooden pegs called dowels that fit tightly into holes drilled in the wood.

TOWN HOUSES

In towns, where space was limited, houses might have several stories. In some towns the upper stories of houses jutted out to give more floor space in upstairs rooms. This shaded the narrow streets below, making them dark and gloomy.

halved or   mortice (left)   joint with holes
trenched   and tenon (right)   for dowels (pegs)

wattle   timber   stone   herringbone
and daub   laths   brick

Medieval builders made the frames using a variety of joints (top). Once the wooden frames were in place, the builders filled the spaces between the timbers. The most commonly used materials were wooden planking, bricks, wattle and daub, timber laths covered in plaster, or plasterwork decorated with paint or swirling patterns, called "pargeting."

Town houses often had space on the
ground floor for a shop. The upper floors
of merchants' houses were used for
storage. The kitchen was sometimes
located in a separate building at the back
of the house to reduce the danger of fire.

WINDOWS

Only a very few houses had glass windows,
which were expensive. They were made of
small panes of glass, each of which had to
be individually blown. The panes were
kept in place by lead beading. Most people
could not afford glass and had wooden
shutters instead. The shutters, which were
closed at night, could be used in the
daytime as tables on which to display
goods.

WASHING

Houses did not have running water or
bathrooms. Toilet arrangements were
simple. Some houses had outside toilets,
which were small sheds over a hole in the
ground. Other houses had toilets in small
upper-story rooms called "garde robes,"
which hung out from the side of the house.

COUNTRY HOUSES

In rural areas, many houses had just one
story. A popular design for larger houses
was the medieval hall. This consisted of a
house built around one very large room
with a massive fireplace that was used for
heating the house and for cooking food.
The ceiling of the hall was very high. Even
so, when the fire was lit the room soon
filled with smoke.

Chimneys were usually built of stone,
and were therefore expensive. Only the
grandest houses had them. It was not until
the late Middle Ages, when bricks were
made in large quantities, that chimneys
became more common.

*Timber-framed houses could be several stories high, especially
where they were built in rows so that each one shared a side
wall with and helped to support the house next door. The
house of a German merchant in the Middle Ages served as a
workshop and storehouse as well as a home. Typically it had
several stories and was roofed with slates, tiles, or thatch.
The large pulley in the center of the house was used for
moving goods easily from floor to floor.*

roof bay   smoke hood   external chimney   internal chimney

*Changing fireplaces and chimneys in the Middle Ages from
the earliest (left) where smoke from an open fire collects in a
roof bay, to the latest (right) with an internal brick chimney.
Chimneys carried smoke out of the house and made it more
practical to add upstairs rooms.*

Francis I came to the throne in 1515. He was said to be a lively, boisterous, extravagant young man described by King Louis XII as a "great boy."

Royal hunts in the time of Francis I often resembled a festive party rather than a sport. Hunters built huge funnel-shaped traps of netting or sailcloth. Then, with a great display of their swords and spears, the huntsmen drove the prey into the trap. Often, ladies of the court participated or watched the spectacle from a distance while the court orchestra played music in the background.

The Loire Valley is one of the most beautiful regions of France. French kings, princes, and nobles have built dozens of castles along the banks of the river. The first were forts, built by the dukes of Anjou to defend their lands from Viking raiders and English armies. Later, as life in France became more settled, the castles were designed more for pleasure than for defense. Perhaps the most beautiful of these châteaux was that built at Chambord by King Francis I.

AN UNPROMISING SITE

The château was built in the heart of a dense forest full of shrubs, thorn bushes, swamps, and marshes. It was a solitary and melancholy place. But the area teemed with wildlife—deer and wild boar wandered in the huge park. It was an ideal site for a royal hunting lodge. Here in 1519, Francis, who was passionately fond of hunting, began building the château.

FAIRY-TALE CASTLE

No one is quite sure who designed Chambord. The superintendent of works, Jean le Breton, was French, but the architects were probably Italian. The design certainly incorporates many features of the Italian Renaissance. Although the overall effect is one of a splendid palace or fairy-tale castle, the actual plan of Chambord (above) is based on that of a fortress. It has a central keep, outer walls, and corner towers, while the entire site is surrounded by a moat. But the outside is embellished with a fantastic selection of turrets, gables, dormer windows, spires, lanterns, and chimneys. Inside, the rooms were decorated with pictures, tapestries, and trophies glorifying hunting.

AN UNCOMFORTABLE HOME

Chambord provided a magnificent backdrop to the hunts, concerts, firework displays, receptions, and balls that were organized to amuse Francis's glittering court. However, while outwardly splendid, the château was far too uncomfortable to be a proper home. Francis I rarely stayed at Chambord for more than three days at a time.

Dancing was a popular pastime at court, and there must have been great celebrations after a successful hunt at Chambord. During Francis's reign the galliard was very popular. This was a very vigorous dance with lots of leaping and kicking.

BUILDING THE CHÂTEAU

Work on Chambord began in 1519. Some 20,000 workers spent 12 years building it before it was abandoned. The statistics of the building are astounding. Chambord is the largest château on the Loire. The front of the building is 420 feet long. There are 440 rooms, and 365 fireplaces, each with its own chimney. There are over 80 staircases, one of which is a double spiral staircase in the center of the château. It is thought to be based on a design by Leonardo da Vinci. Although the roof today is gray slate, it was originally decorated with gilded lead. Around the château is a huge forest enclosed by a wall that—at 20 miles—is the longest property fence in France.

INFLUENTIAL OWNERS

The château bears the stamp of some of the important people who lived or stayed there. The biggest influence is that of Francis I, the builder, whose salamander emblem decorates many parts of the building. He died in 1547, before some parts of the château, including the chapel,

were completed. His son, Henry II, continued the work. Louis XIV (1638–1715), the most powerful king of France, created magnificent state apartments in the main part of the château. Other famous inhabitants included Stanislas, the exiled king of Poland, whose son-in-law, King Louis XV, ordered the chapel to be decorated, and Maurice de Saxe, one of France's most famous soldiers.

This beautiful picture of Chambord is a decoration on a Sèvres vase ordered by King Charles X in about 1823.

31

One of the most beautiful rooms in Chambord was the bedroom of Marie Thérèse, wife of Louis XIV (right). The northeast corner of the château contains Francis I's bedroom and study, which were decorated with salamanders (his own emblem), fleurs-de-lys, and the arms of France. These devices can be seen when the see-through page is turned. Francis's bedroom, on the first floor of the tower (below), must have been one of the coldest rooms in the castle. Francis himself may have carved some graffiti near the window, which reads "Woman is fickle."

DESERTED AND BARE

The château could not be heated and was never furnished completely. Apart from the occasional caretaker, Chambord remained cold and empty for a large part of its life, reviving only during the occasional royal visit. It was eventually abandoned. An inventory of furniture at Chambord taken in 1685 records that the only furniture in the 400 rooms was one red velvet armchair, 30 ordinary chairs, some folding chairs, one red velvet couch, 18 stools, eight mirrors, six basins, four chamber pots, 40 chandeliers (18 of which were broken), and 13 tables.

1 **Bedroom of Francis I**
2 **Cabinet (study and chapel) of Francis I**
3 **Louis XIV's apartment**
4 **Bedroom of Marie Thérèse, wife of Louis XIV**
5 **Tapestry room containing scenes of Francis I hunting**
6 **Maurice de Saxe's drawing room**

IMPROVEMENTS

Chambord was never quite forgotten. Later kings and other owners made improvements and added new buildings to the original. During the 18th century, Chambord was occupied first by Louis XV's parents-in-law, and then by Maurice de Saxe and his entire regiment. Maurice spent a large fortune on the palace and lived there like a king. He even converted one hall to a theater with 1,800 seats. Later, Chambord was looted during the French Revolution. After that, its various owners were unable to repair the building. The château was bought by the French government in 1930. Since then millions of francs have been spent to restore it to its former glory.

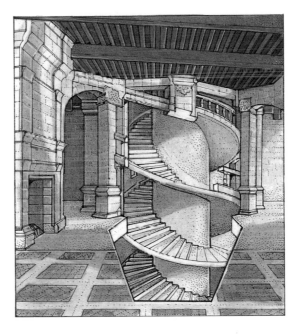

The two spirals of the great staircase wind, one above the other, around the same central shaft. This shaft is pierced with openings so that people on different staircases can see each other without ever meeting. This makes the staircase majestic and fun at the same time. The spiral rises through three large cross-shaped halls that were used for concerts and balls. The staircase is crowned by a lantern over 65 feet above the ground floor. The top picture also shows one of four stoves that were installed in the cross-shaped room on the first floor by Maurice de Saxe.

7   Hall converted to a theater by Maurice de Saxe
8   Guard room
9   Trophy room
10 Double spiral staircase
11 Louis XIV's billiard room
12 Corridor
13 Chapel completed by Louis XV for King Stanislas

By the end of the Middle Ages, a great network of trade routes covered Europe and Asia. The merchants who traveled these long and often dangerous routes, hundreds of miles from their own homes, needed safe places to stay.

CARAVANSERAI

Among the most impressive of these resting places for travelers were the "caravanserai." They were built throughout the Middle East beginning in the 1200s. They provided not only a safe place to eat and sleep, but every conceivable service a traveler might need. They even became some travelers' homes for a while.

The caravanserai of Aminābādh (above and left) was shaped like an octagonal fortress with a central well. The tall walls provided defense against all but an army. The stables were located around the inside wall, facing into the courtyard.

SMALL BEGINNINGS

The earliest caravanserai were simply walled enclosures protecting a well. Many caravanserai were built in the mountains, and were generally small and simple in design. They had a large central hall with arched aisles at the edges. A long bench running down the center of the hall provided a sleeping or sitting place. Animals usually had to be left in stables outside the walls because there was rarely a central courtyard.

But gradually the role of caravanserai grew more important. The Seljuk rulers of Turkey built a large number of them. Caravanserai made trading easier and safer, and ultimately brought great wealth to the country. By 1300, many caravanserai had grown into large buildings or even small communities. For the weary traveler far from home, the sight of these early motels must have been comforting.

This map shows some of the main trade routes used by Arab traders. The backbone of the system was the Great Silk Road, which linked China with Europe.

LOCATION

Caravanserai were built either along highways or in towns, often a day's journey apart. Many caravanserai, especially in more remote areas, were like fortresses surrounded by walls and guarded by towers. Inside, the weary traveler could sleep on raised platforms in communal halls. In larger caravanserai there might be a second story containing luxurious bedrooms or flat roofs where people could sleep.

The traveler might also find storerooms where goods could be stowed safely, a dining room like a café, a washing fountain or bathhouse, a blacksmith and a leather worker who could repair damaged equipment, different-sized stables for pack animals (such as camels, donkeys, and mules) and for saddle animals such as horses. Each caravanserai was managed by a warden. Many of the services provided were free, paid for by the state.

Inside the walls, traders could rest, feed and water their animals, and relax for a while. By traveling in caravans, the traders protected themselves and each other from bandit attacks. Some caravans were very large and there were several that contained over 5,000 camels.

TOWN CARAVANSERAI

Some caravanserai, especially those along the most important trade routes, were enormous. They had shops, bakeries, kitchens, refectories (dining halls), mosques, and hospitals inside the walls. The huge caravanserai at Aliabad even had a flour mill and two ice houses in it!

Many of the caravanserai located in towns developed into important trading centers in their own right. These caravanserai were often built close to bazaars and were originally designed as depots. They had large warehouses where many different types of goods were stored in bales and packing cases at their journey's end, awaiting sale. Before long, the merchants who stayed in the caravanserai began to trade inside the caravanserai walls. As a result many of these caravanserai, which were sometimes called "dars," grew into markets. Some became famous for selling particular goods, such as oil and soap.

This illustration, made about A.D. 1250, shows a caravan traveling to Mecca. The traders announce their progress with drums and trumpets.

35

A MAORI PA

During the first 1,000 years A.D., the Polynesians settled on the islands of the Pacific. One of the last areas of the Pacific to be settled was what is now New Zealand. This was reached by the Maoris sometime during the 900s. The land must have seemed like a paradise for the first settlers, who were able to build their homes wherever they wanted.

Maori houses often had roofs made from bundles of branches. These were laid on top of each other to form a waterproof thatch. The walls were made of panels of branches. Immediately below is a sleeping house. Bottom left is a larger house. Notice the earth bank along the side.

COMPETITION

Before the Maoris arrived, New Zealand's two islands had been uninhabited. The first settlers were able to live well by hunting and gathering food. But within a relatively short time, the settlers had hunted many of the animals close to extinction. As the stock of animals shrank, and the human population increased, so did competition for food. The Maoris began to develop agriculture and set about defending their food resources from other tribes.

HOMES FOR SAFETY

By about 1350, tribal warfare had become common in the north island. The Maoris who lived there began to build their homes in easily defensible places. Favorite sites were in swamps, on rocky outcrops, and on the rims of extinct volcanoes. The Maoris improved the natural defenses of the sites with earthworks, ditches, and palisades (fences). In this way they created fortified villages, called "pa," which were similar to the hill forts built by Iron Age people in Europe. Some pa had very elaborate defenses consisting of interlocking mazes of ditches and banks. In the center of the pa was a palisade made of tree trunks, shaped into stakes with stone or obsidian tools. The stakes were sharpened and their tips hardened by fire. Inside the palisade was the main village, which consisted of homes and storehouses.

SLEEPING HOUSES

We don't know very much about the houses the Maoris built inside the pa. From the archaeological evidence, it seems likely that there were two types of buildings. The most common were small, squarish houses. From the remains of bedding material found inside them, such as twigs and leaves, it seems that many of these smaller houses were used as sleeping quarters.

LARGE HOUSES

Each pa also seems to have had at least one very large house in it. One of these large houses, found at Tiromoana pa in Hawke's Bay, was over 36 feet long and nearly 13 feet wide. This house had a pitched roof with a ridge held up by center posts. The eaves of the roof were very long and overhung a low earth bank built along the base of the walls. This bank probably made the houses more weatherproof.

The main frame of these larger houses was made from poles, or sometimes planks, which must have been shaped from tree trunks with stone tools. The walls were made from small stakes and narrow planks. Some large houses had one or more hearth pits dug in the earth floor.

CHIEFS

It seems likely that the large houses belonged to tribal chiefs. The size of each house may have indicated the power of the chief who lived in it. The houses were probably used as places for assembly and discussion. We also know, from the diaries and log books of European sailors who went to New Zealand, that the large houses were used for receiving guests. It is probable that some of the houses may even have been specially built as guest houses for visitors. From eyewitness accounts it seems that many of the houses were richly decorated with carvings but, to date, no examples have been found.

Many pa were similar to the one shown here. It is protected by a palisade of sharpened stakes and platforms on which the defenders stood to hurl weapons.

Large houses were decorated with carvings (below). The carving on the far side of the door of this modern meeting house (far left) is a self-portrait of the carver.

ZULU HOMES

A Zulu food pot. The Zulus' staple foods were millet and maize. These were ground into flour on a concave stone and made into porridge.

The Zulu are an ancient people. They are the descendants of a wandering group of Bantu people who lived by herding cattle and farming. They settled in Zululand in about A.D. 1000, long before any European settlers came to Africa. Their new homeland was fertile, watered by several large rivers, and free of the tsetse flies that infected and killed livestock in many other parts of Africa. The Zulus had to fight to keep their precious land. As a result, they became one of the most powerful and warlike nations in Africa.

A FAMILY HOME

The focus of Zulu life was the homestead or "umuzi." The umuzi was surrounded by a circular fence of thick posts or brushwood and had three entrances. In the center of the umuzi was an enclosure for penning cattle at night.

A typical umuzi contained several huts, each the home of a single family of parents and their unmarried children. A headman, called an "induna," ruled the umuzi. The induna's hut was always opposite the main entrance of the umuzi. Around this hut were the huts of his wives, arranged according to seniority. The huts of his unmarried sons were close to the entrance.

Inside a Zulu hut, food is being cooked over an open fire. The furnishing of the hut is spartan, with just a few mats on the floor, and pots for cooking and storage.

BEEHIVE HUTS

Each hut was built in the shape of a beehive. The framework was made from flexible saplings driven deep into the ground and tied together with grass rope. Woven grass mats were then laid over the framework and fastened into place with grass ropes pulled over the top. The mats were overlapped to make the roof rainproof.

Each hut had an arched doorway. This was so low it had to be entered on hands and knees. It was closed by a removable door made from woven branches, which could be "locked" by a pole lashed to the outside.

COOL HOMES

The grass thatch of the roof allowed some wind to pass right through the hut. This kept the interior of the hut cool, and blew the smoke away from the fire. The floor was made from cow dung and mud, often dirt taken from an ant hill and mixed with water to make a kind of cement. When it dried, the surface was polished with animal fat until it shone like marble.

With cattle feeding solely on grass, the dung is merely a pulp which is practically odorless and soon dries out. . . . This point is stressed because Europeans cannot understand why cow dung is used . . . to smear frequently the earth-floors of huts, schools, and churches.

— *E. A. Ritter* —

FURNISHINGS

Inside the huts, there were very few furnishings. Domestic items, such as rush sleeping mats and animal-skin blankets, pots, and bags of tobacco, were hung from the sides of the hut.

Meals were a formal occasion. Before eating, the Zulus washed their hands and faces in a special clay basin. The families were seated with the men on one side, the women on the other, and the eldest people nearest the door. Meals were eaten from a common food dish. Each person ate with his or her own wooden spoon, which was placed with its bowl resting on the rim of the dish and its handle on the floor.

The umuzi was designed as both a fortified village and a cattle pen. Status was indicated by the position of the hut inside the umuzi. The huts of the most important people were farthest from the entrance. Cattle were the main wealth of the Zulus. In a region where wood is scarce, "cakes" made of dried cow dung were used as fuel for the fires.

Stages in the construction of a Zulu hut (left to right). The design uses local building materials to produce a practical shelter. The Zulu men, who were warriors and cattle herders, built the huts. Women did everything else, including cooking, cleaning, craftwork, and most of the farming.

WEAVERS' COTTAGES

Before 1750 in the Western world, many workers' houses were both their homes and workplaces. Goods such as nails, shoes, and wool cloth were made in rooms in workers' houses or in workshops in their backyards.

CLOTH PRODUCTION

The cloth industry was typical of this method of production. In those days many people stayed at home to work and the whole family was involved in producing cloth. Different members of the family prepared the wool by carding (combing), spinning, and weaving it by hand.

LOOM SHOPS

Weavers who kept their looms at home were called "first hands." Each weaver's cottage had spinning wheels and a loom for weaving. Since weaving was the most skilled job and the loom was the biggest piece of equipment, the needs of the weaver affected the design of the cottage.

1 Hearth
2 Raw wool
3 "Cards" for combing wool
4 Spinning wheel
5 Loom
6 Finished cloth ready for market

Many farmers and their families earned extra money by carding (combing), spinning, and weaving in their homes (below). Wool merchants supplied the raw wool and collected the finished cloth to sell in their own shops or at nearby markets. Many merchants, who wanted their workers to live in the same area, built special cottages for them (right).

THE MAIN ROOMS

The weaver's loom was kept in a room called a loom shop. The loom shop might be bigger than all the bedrooms put together. Spare rooms were often rented out to other weavers. This meant that weavers' cottages were generally very crowded, so in many homes the children slept in the ground-floor rooms.

The house also had one or two bedrooms, a kitchen, a living room, and a scullery. Houses did not have running water or bathrooms, so water had to be collected from the village pump or stream. Most people washed in the kitchen (which was the warmest room) using a jug and bowl, or in a wooden or tin bathtub. People cleaned their teeth with salt or even brick dust. Soap was expensive, so dishes and cutlery were also scrubbed with sand, brick dust, or salt to get them clean.

HOUSEWORK

The cottages were very hard to keep clean. The wood or coal fires that heated them produced a huge amount of soot. Most cottages had bare floorboards or stone floors that needed regular sweeping with heather or twig brooms. Any rugs had to be taken outside and beaten to get rid of the soot and dust, or brushed with damp tea leaves to absorb the dirt.

1 **Loom**
2 **Loom shop**
3 **Bedroom**
4 **Kitchen and dining room**
5 **Scullery**
6 **Pantry**
7 **Toilet**
8 **Passage between houses**

The cloth merchants who owned the weavers' cottages usually built them joined together in long rows, called terraces, to save money. The cottages were usually two stories high. The loom shop could be on any floor, and always had very wide windows. This was to let plenty of light in so that the weavers could see their work clearly. The toilet was in a small hut behind the cottage. The seat was made from wooden planks with a circle cut in them, placed over a bucket or a hole in the ground. The sewage was sometimes spread on the land as fertilizer.

PORT SUNLIGHT

Many factory workers lived in deplorable conditions in European industrial towns in the 19th century (below). Port Sunlight (bottom) was William Lever's attempt to build a new factory and provide the best possible living conditions for his employees. It is shown here in 1898, when only the factory and the first set of houses had been completed.

The rapid growth of towns during the Industrial Revolution meant a great increase in the number of squalid slum houses. In England, one rich industrialist, William Lever, felt it was his duty to improve the living conditions of his workers. When Lever ordered the building of a new soap factory in 1888, he also built a whole new village for workers.

It is my hope . . . to build houses in which our workpeople will be able to live and be comfortable. [With] semi-detached houses, with gardens back and front . . . they will learn that there is more enjoyment in life than in the mere going to and returning from work . . .

— *William Lever* —

PLANNING PORT SUNLIGHT

Lever's architects designed not only houses for the workers to rent, but also a hospital, art gallery, gymnasium, swimming pool, theater, and social clubs. Although this was unusual, many industrialists and architects before Lever had planned and built houses for their workers, and some had provided leisure facilities, too. But the houses had mostly been packed tightly into terraces, with few open spaces between. Port Sunlight was different because it combined good-quality industrial houses with pleasant open spaces.

THE HOUSES

The designs of the houses were relatively simple. The only unusual feature was that every house had an indoor bathroom. Two main designs were developed. The "Kitchen Cottage" was the simplest, with a kitchen, scullery, pantry, and three bedrooms. The "Parlor Cottage" was larger, with a parlor and a fourth bedroom.

The decoration of the earliest homes, built before 1890, is quite plain. Later houses had more complicated decoration, with molded and twisted chimneys, carved woodwork and stone, pargeting (decorated plasterwork), and leaded windows. Lever said his architects had become "more and more elaborate in architectural design, and more and more extravagant in the use of costly building materials."

BLOCKS

Most of the houses were simpler. They were arranged in blocks consisting of between 2 and 18 cottages. Each house was built at least 16 feet from the nearest road, and all had front yards. Each block covered a large area. Some of the space was divided into backyards where, hidden from public sight, householders could hang their laundry out to dry. Some of the space was made into gardens, which Lever believed were important. He even had playgrounds designed for children.

These are three-bedroom "Kitchen Cottages," with neat front gardens. Although actually built to similar designs, the houses in different blocks had distinctive external features that made them look very different from each other.

A "New Rapid" geyser (water heater) of 1884 similar to those fitted in some houses at Port Sunlight. Running hot water was found mainly in the homes of the very rich and was a real luxury for working people.

This scene shows the parlor in one of the larger cottages. Lever believed that badly built houses soon became slums and that working people would be proud to live in and look after well-built homes. Port Sunlight was an experiment that proved this idea to be correct.

UNUSUAL DESIGNS

Two unusual designs were cottages built to look like the birthplace of the playwright William Shakespeare, or like a timber-framed hall.

There had also been plans to build houses in styles representing the countries in which Lever's company had factories. However, only one such block was built, in a Flemish style using Belgian bricks.

A MODEL ESTATE

Port Sunlight caused a sensation. The estate received a flood of distinguished visitors, including England's king and queen. Originally there were 28 houses. The village now contains 850 houses, as well as 72 apartments, which are still occupied. Throughout its history Port Sunlight has been modernized with the installation of electricity, gas, and many other improvements. The design of the village, particularly its emphasis on well-built houses standing in green spaces, greatly influenced town planning throughout the 20th century.

43

BIOSPHERE 2

Thousands of square feet of glass enclose Biosphere 2's seven environments. These include an ocean with a coral reef, a river, a rain forest, a marsh, a desert, a savannah, and living quarters for the humans who live inside.

High on a plateau in the Arizona desert sits what is perhaps the most unusual and expensive home on earth. The building, which is made mainly of glass and steel, covers 3.15 acres and cost over $150 million to build.

SEALED INSIDE

Biosphere 2 is a giant laboratory built to study how the earth's ecosystem works and to examine the problems of colonizing outer space. It is a completely airtight, self-contained environment. Once inside, the eight people who lived in it for two years had to produce their own food. They even relied on the interaction of the plants and animals in the Biosphere to produce enough oxygen for them to breathe.

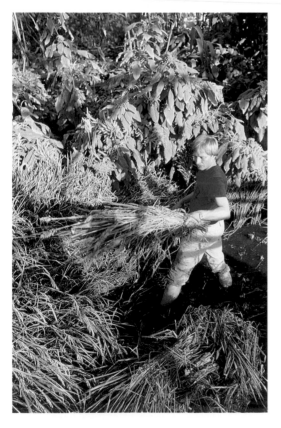

One of the Biospherians harvesting rice in the agricultural biome, one of the seven environments enclosed inside Biosphere 2.

BUILDING MATERIALS

Biosphere 2 looks like a gigantic greenhouse. It is made of a steel space frame covered in glass panels that are sealed to make the building airtight. The series of buildings that make up the Biosphere stand on thick concrete foundations. A special lining and a massive underground barrier made of stainless steel prevent air and water inside the buildings from escaping through the ground.

All the materials used in the Biosphere had to be free of toxic substances that might pollute the sensitive ecosystems. All metal surfaces, for example, were painted with polyester resins to prevent polluting the environment inside.

SELF-SUFFICIENCY

The closed environment of the Biosphere was intended to be a kind of 20th-century Noah's Ark. It was planned that each of the small environments would be self-sufficient. Each part would also help to maintain life in the other parts. People and plants would exchange oxygen and carbon dioxide, and wastes would be used as fertilizers. Damp air from the ocean area would provide moisture for the swamp, and plants and animals would be food for each other.

ENVIRONMENTS

Biosphere 2 houses over 3,800 plant and animal species in seven separate ecological areas, or "biomes." These represent the main natural environments found on Biosphere 1, the earth. The human biome, which is over 11,500 square feet, contained an observatory, a library, a communications center with telephone and computer connections to the outside, a gym, a dining hall, and eight separate sleeping apartments, all housed inside a white dome. The four male and four female Biospherians were sealed inside Biosphere 2 for two years. While they lived inside the Biosphere they farmed the land in the agricultural biome and performed a great variety of scientific experiments.

ARTIFICIAL WEATHER

Biosphere 2 is not large enough to have natural weather inside it, so machines help to simulate this. Over 3,500 sensors feed data to the computer-controlled heaters and coolers that balance the temperature and the pumps that direct the flow of water and air around the buildings. A giant pair of rubber lungs helps to equalize the air pressure in different parts of the Biosphere to prevent the glass walls from exploding or imploding.

PROBLEMS

On September 27, 1993, eight pale and thin people emerged from Biosphere 2. During their two-year stay in the ecosystem they had all lost weight and had had to deal with many problems. The plants were unable to produce enough oxygen, and sometimes air had to be pumped in from outside to keep the people and animals alive. Insects ate many of the crops, and some of the animals, including the bees and hummingbirds, died. Some of the Biospherians became sick, suffering from skin diseases among other illnesses.

LESSONS FOR THE FUTURE

Despite these setbacks, Biosphere 2 did support eight humans and several thousands of other species. The recycling systems worked well. Although it received some criticism, the project has helped us better understand how humans might live in closer harmony with nature. Perhaps it can teach us how to build better homes in the future or even make the colonization of outer space a more practical possibility.

One of the Biospherians tending the goats. Goats are very efficient milk producers and eat less than cows. Although Biosphere 2 was supposed to be completely self-sufficient, the project had problems with oxygen levels and the food supply.

Mealtime in the Biosphere. This is a typical meal eaten by the Biospherians during the two-year experiment.

This list of key dates includes some of the major inventions and developments in the methods humans have used to make their homes. Dates before A.D. 1400 are approximate.

Tepees are the traditional homes of the Plains Indians of North America. They are made of buffalo hides over a frame of strong poles. They were designed to be put up and taken down quickly, so that the tribe could follow the herds. The Indians hung their possessions, weapons, and medicine bags inside the tepee around the walls. Smoke flaps at the top of the tepee could be closed to keep the heat in or opened to let the smoke from the fire out.

B.C.

25,000 Stone Age artists paint inside their caves. People take first steam baths by throwing water over rocks heated in a fire.

24,000 Hut building is a well-established skill. The first huts are lean-tos with skin and brushwood supported on branches.

14,000 Round, stone-walled huts with sunken floors become common in the Middle East. Square, hide-covered huts are built in South America.

7,000 Wattle and daub (mud plastered on woven branches) becomes a common building material in Europe.

6,000 The Chinese build round wooden huts with sunken floors.

4,000 The first known building with decorated walls is built in Mesopotamia.

3,000 Large communal meeting houses are built in China out of wood and thatch.

3,000 The first high-backed chairs are used in Egypt. Ancient Egyptians also invent the bathroom, and a form of concrete.

2,000 The first door lock is made near Nineveh in Assyria.

1,200 Pacific islanders build wooden houses on stilts close to the shoreline.

150 Romans discover that volcanic dust found near Vesuvius sets hard when mixed with lime and water. They call it *cementium*. The Romans also mass-produce fired bricks and invent central heating (the hypocaust) and the rounded arch.

A.D.

250 The squinch is invented in the Middle East. This allows domed roofs to be built more easily.

1463 The first reported numbering of houses is introduced in Paris.

1589 The first flushing toilet is invented by Sir John Harrington.

1716 Swedish engineer Martin Triewald invents hot water central heating.

1799 First gas fire demonstrated in France.

1824 Joseph Aspidin patents modern synthetic cement.

1885 The world's first skyscraper, the 10-story Chicago Home Insurance Building, is erected.

Glossary

bitumen: a naturally occurring tarry substance.

brazier: a pan that holds burning coals or wood.

citadel: a fortress overlooking a city.

Cro-Magnons: prehistoric humans, who lived in Europe, Asia, and Africa from about 35,000 to 8,000 B.C.

dormer window: window projecting from a sloping roof.

eaves: the overhanging edges of a roof.

foundations: the base of a building, usually under the ground, which is designed to carry the building's weight.

gable: the triangular upper part of a wall at the end of a ridged roof.

Ice Age: a period when ice sheets cover large regions of the earth. Ice Ages occur periodically. The last Ice Age began about 1¾ million years ago.

lantern: a construction, with windows, that covers a room or dome.

lath: a narrow strip of wood, nailed to a rafter, that provides a base for shingles or tiles.

Neanderthals: prehistoric humans who lived in Europe, Africa, and Asia from about 100,000 to 35,000 years ago.

obsidian: a kind of natural glass formed by volcanoes.

pargeting: ornamental plasterwork.

relief: a panel with a carving on it.

skyscraper: a building built around, and whose weight is supported by, a steel frame. This allows the building to be many stories higher than one whose weight is supported by walls.

squinch: a half-dome built across the corner of a square chamber to make it octagonal. This allows a dome to be more easily built over it.

Stone Age: the period during which people used stone tools. The Stone Age began about 2.5 million years ago. About 3,000 B.C., bronze tools were developed in the Middle East.

terra-cotta: hard, unglazed pottery that is usually brownish-red in color.

wattle and daub: a building material made from panels of thin woven branches plastered with mud or a similar substance.

Quotations

The marriage blessing is based on Indian inscriptions dating from shortly after the fall of Mohenjo-Daro. The Egyptian inscription is one of many pieces of "wise advice" from ancient Egypt. Juvenal (about A.D. 55–138), was a soldier, a priest, and a lawyer. He is most famous for his *Satires*— writings that made attacks on corruption and the follies of ancient Rome. E. A. Ritter grew up among the Zulus in Natal. The description comes from his book *Shaka's Zulu*. Industrialist William Lever (1851–1925) became rich through manufacturing and selling soap.

INDEX